Celebrating Cultures

Powwow

Jill Foran

WEIGL PUBLISHERS INC.

Published by Weigl Publishers Inc.
123 South Broad Street, Box 227
Mankato, MN, 56002, USA
Web site: www.weigl.com

Library of Congress Cataloging-in-Publication Data

Foran, Jill.
  Powwow / by Jill Foran.
      p. cm. -- (Celebrating cultures)
Includes index.
Summary: Provides information on the Native American celebratory
gatherings known as powwows.
  ISBN 1-59036-095-8 (lib. bdg. : alk. paper)
  1. Powwows--Juvenile literature. [1. Powwows. 2. Festivals.] I.
Title.
  E98.P86 F67 2003
  399--dc21
                            2002014565

Printed in the United States of America
1 2 3 4 5 6 7 8 9 0   06 05 04 03 02

Project Coordinator Janice Redlin **Design & Layout** Bryan Pezzi
Copy Editor Michael Lowry **Photo Researcher** Wendy Cosh

Photograph Credits

Every reasonable effort has been made to trace ownership and to obtain permission to reprint copyright material.
The publishers would be pleased to have any errors or omissions brought to their attention so that they may be
corrected in subsequent printings.

Cover: Native-American Powwow (Marilyn "Angel" Wynn); **Corel Corporation:** page 5R; **Denver Public Library,
Western History Collection:** pages 7T, 7B; **Dominique Dobson:** page 13TM; **PhotoSpin, Inc.:** pages 13TL, 21,
22; **Marilyn "Angel" Wynn:** pages 3, 4, 5L, 6, 8, 9L, 9R, 10, 11T, 11B, 12T, 12B, 13TR, 13B, 14, 15L, 15R, 16L, 16R,
17L, 17R, 18, 19L, 19R.

Contents

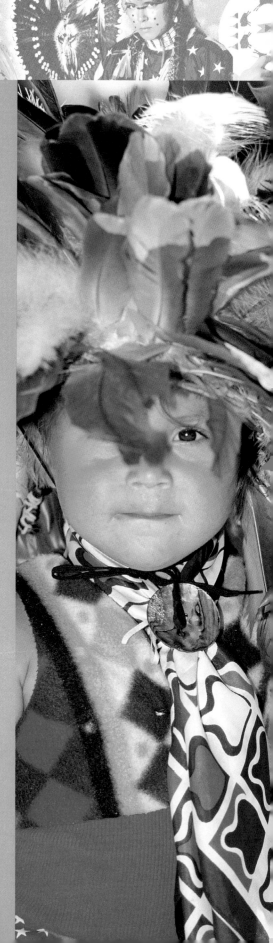

Special Gatherings

People gather to dance and sing at powwows.

Native Americans hold special gatherings throughout the United States. They are called powwows. Powwows allow Native **nations** to join together and celebrate their cultures. Native Americans honor their shared **traditions** at powwows. They gather to dance and sing with old friends. They also make new friends at powwows.

Native Americans use powwows to help preserve their history.

Powwows usually occur on weekends. Outdoor powwows are held across the country during spring and summer. Powwows may be indoors in the colder months. These gatherings take place almost every weekend of the year in the United States.

Powwows are held in many places. They can be held in campgrounds, community halls, cultural centers, or on traditional lands.

Native Americans of all ages enjoy powwows.

Ancient Ceremonies

People met to dance and tell stories.

Today's powwows can be traced back to ancient Native-American celebrations. For thousands of years, Native Americans have gathered to tell stories, play music, and dance. These gatherings were held at different times of the year. When European **missionaries** came to North America, they encouraged people to hold their celebrations on **Christian** religious days. These celebrations led to modern powwows.

Celebrations, such as this Dance Gathering, are a longstanding Native-American tradition.

The early Plains nations held some of the liveliest dancing ceremonies. These nations included the Pawnee and the Poncha. Many of the special songs and dances seen at today's powwows come from the Pawnee and the Poncha.

The word "powwow" comes from the Algonquian word "pauwau." A pauwau was a large gathering of medicine men and religious leaders.

Members of the Plains nations dress in traditional clothing when they dance.

Powwows of the Past

The original dances were performed by warriors.

The powwow tradition is more than 100 years old. The original dances were performed by **warriors**. The dances were performed when the warriors hunted or fought successfully. More people became involved with these gatherings over time. The powwows helped draw groups of Native Americans together. More than thirty Plains nations were holding powwows by the late 1800s.

Native-American nations have gathered together to feast for many years.

Speeches, gift giving, and feasts were added to the festivities. Native-American dancers and singers from different nations joined together to teach each other new songs and dances. Over the years, these new dance styles and songs began to blend together.

In the 1920s, dance and song contests became a part of powwows. The best performers won prizes.

The khouse root is just one of the traditional foods that are served at powwows.

Powwows of the Present

Many families travel to powwows across the country.

Many Native-American families go on the powwow **circuit** during the warmer months. This means that they travel to powwows across the country. At the powwows, dancers and drum groups perform in a large circular area. This area is called an arena. Family members of the performers sit in the audience in seats around the arena.

Some celebrations, such as this one, are called Friendship Gatherings.

The sound of the drum is considered the heartbeat of many Native-American ceremonies. The drum has a large, wooden frame that is covered with **rawhide**. Performers strike the drum with drumsticks. Then, they sing and blend their voices with the drumbeats.

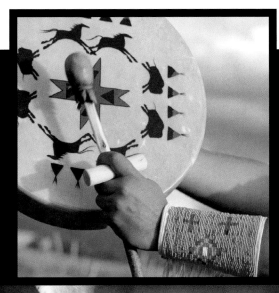

The Native Americans believe that the spirit of the drum maker is inside every drum made.

There are two kinds of powwows. There are competition powwows and traditional powwows. Dancers and drum groups compete for prize money at competition powwows. Dancers and drum groups do not compete at traditional powwows. Instead, they receive gifts.

The beating of a drum is very important to Native-American culture.

Americans Celebrate

Hundreds of powwows are held in the United States each year. Native Americans from across the country travel to these celebrations. The map below highlights some of the powwows in the United States.

The Crow Fair is held every August at Crow Agency, Montana. It features lively dancing and singing. Delicious foods and beautiful crafts are sold at the fair.

The Acorn Festival and Powwow is held every September in Tuolomne, California. This powwow features a **handgame** tournament.

Crow Agency

Nebraska

Tuolomne

Albuquerque

For more than 135 years, the Homecoming Winnebago Powwow in Nebraska has honored the Native Americans who have served in wars.

In early spring, many of the country's best Native-American singers and dancers take part in the Ann Arbor Powwow in Michigan.

In Oklahoma City, Oklahoma, more than 1,200 Native-American dancers perform at the Red Earth Annual Celebration. This powwow is one of the largest Native-American dance celebrations in the country.

Ann Arbor

N

Oklahoma City

The Gathering of Nations Powwow is held in Albuquerque, New Mexico. It is the largest powwow in North America. More than 3,000 Native-American dancers and singers attend the powwow.

0   250   500 miles

A Grand Beginning

Powwows begin with the Grand Entry.

Powwows begin with the Grand Entry. Spectators stand during this ceremony. An **eagle staff** and the flags of Native-American nations are brought into the arena. Hosts, **elders**, honored guests, and dancers enter the arena next. When all of the dancers have gathered, everyone is silent. The **flag song** is played. Soon, the dancing will begin.

The Grand Entry is a spectacular event filled with excitement.

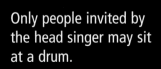

Etiquette is a very important part of powwow culture. Singers share their songs with each other. However, singers should not sing another group's song without permission. There are also rules for drum circles. Only the drummers can sit around the drum. The singers must stand behind the drummers.

The head singer provides all of the songs at a powwow. The head singer also leads the other members of the drum circle.

Only people invited by the head singer may sit at a drum.

A Reason to Dance

Dancers move in a crouched position in Traditional Dance.

The Traditional Dance is one of the most common dance styles. It honors the skills of traditional hunters and warriors. Some dancers move in a crouched position. They pretend to track or hunt.

The Grass Dance developed out of an early warrior dance. Grass dancers wear outfits with long pieces of yarn attached. As the dancers weave and step, the yarn sways like long pieces of grass.

The Traditional Dance is the oldest form of dance in Native-American culture.

The Grass Dance reflects warrior movements such as stalking and fighting.

The Fancy Dance is known for its quick steps and fast turns. It is the newest of the dance styles. Fancy dancers must be very fit. They perform many jumps and twirls.

The Jingle-dress Dance requires great skill. The dancers wear outfits that are decorated with little metal cones. As the dancers move to the beat of the drum, these cones jingle to the beat. Usually, only women and girls perform this dance.

Dancers always dance in a circle at powwows. Most Native-American nations believe that the circle is a **symbol** of life.

An adult jingle dress has between 400 and 700 cones on it.

The Fancy dancer wears a headdress with two eagle feathers.

Regalia and Gifts

Every dance style has a different style of outfit.

Regal Regalia

The dance outfits are a very important part of powwows. Every style of dance has a different style of outfit. Fancy dancers wear brightly colored outfits with two feather **bustles** tied to their backs. Dance outfits are decorated with a variety of materials. These include leather, porcupine quills, beads, and fur. The outfits at powwows are called regalia.

Regalia is often made up of treasured gifts from people in the dancer's life.

Giving Away the Giveaways

Special people may be honored for different reasons at powwows. It could be a birthday, a graduation, or even a wedding. The person does not receive gifts. Instead, the person being honored gives gifts to everyone else. This is a way for the person to thank everyone who supported them. These gifts are called giveaways.

Dancing regalia is very personal. It is often designed to reflect the dancer's thoughts and emotions. A dancer's regalia changes as the dancer grows and changes.

Dancers will add to their outfit throughout their lives.

Bustles are made from feathers that are grouped together in a circular pattern.

For More Information

Many books and Web sites help to explain the history and traditions of the powwow. To learn more about powwows, you can borrow books from a library or search the Internet.

Books

Read these books to learn more about powwows and Native-American culture.

Left Hand Bull, Jacqueline. *Lakota Hoopdancer*. New York: Dutton Children's Books, 1999.

Greene, Jacqueline D. *Powwow: A Good Day to Dance*. New York: Franklin Watts Inc., 1999.

Web Sites

For information on every aspect of a powwow, visit: www.powwows.com

To learn more about the dancing and traditions of Native Americans, type such terms as "powwow" or "drum circle" into an online encyclopedia, such as Encarta.
www.encarta.com

Imagine if...

A powwow dancer's outfit is very important. The outfit shows the dancer's thoughts and feelings. Imagine that you have been invited to dance at a powwow. What would your dancing outfit look like? How would it reflect your own thoughts and feelings? Design and draw a picture of your dancing outfit. How is your outfit different than the outfits shown in this book? How is your outfit the same? Make a list of the differences and similarities.

What You Have Learned

1 Powwows are held throughout North America.

2 Today's powwow traditions come from ancient Native-American celebrations.

3 The two types of powwows are competition powwows and traditional powwows.

4 Dancers and drummers perform in a circular area called an arena.

5 There are four main types of dances at powwows. They are the Fancy Dance, Grass Dance, Traditional Dance, and Jingle-dress Dance.

6 Dancing outfits are called regalia.

More Facts to Know

- Not all Native-American nations celebrate powwows.

- The powwow committee is responsible for organizing all powwow events.

- The Master of Ceremonies (MC) runs the powwow. The MC decides when each dance will be held.

- Most powwows have a head male and a head female dancer. These dancers are models for all the other dancers.

- Special booths are set up outside the powwow arena. The booths sell arts, crafts, and delicious foods.

- Children as young as 10 months old have competed in powwow dances.

Words to Know

bustles: bunches of feathers

Christian: a person who believes Jesus is the son of God

circuit: a route that is regularly traveled

eagle staff: a tall stick that represents all of the Native-American nations

elders: older members of a nation

etiquette: rules of correct behavior

flag song: a song that honors the flags carried in the Grand Entry

handgame: a traditional Native-American stick game

missionaries: people who teach religion in other countries

nations: Native-American peoples or groups

rawhide: skin of cattle or other animals

symbol: something that represents something else

traditions: customs passed down from parents to children

warriors: people who fight in battles

Index